Stories in Stone

THE WORLD OF ANIMAL FOSSILS

by JO S. KITTINGER

A First Book

Franklin Watts
A Division of Grolier Publishing
New York London Hong Kong Sydney Danbury, Connecticut

For Rick,
who loves fossils, rocks, minerals,
and me.

Photographs ©: Dinosaur State Park: 9; George C. Page Museum: 53, 54, 55, 57; Jay Mallin: 34; Jo S. Kittinger: 33; Museum of the Rockies: 38, 46 (Bruce Selyem); Paleontologicae Research Institute: 29, 4 (Steven Hellevy), 1, 4 inset, 5, 16, 18, 21, 24, 26, 36, 42, 48 (Wendy Taylor); Photo Researchers: 22, 50 (James L. Amos), 8 (Scott Camazine), 13, 41 (Francois Gohier), 6 (Sylvain Grendadam), 32 (Tom McHugh/National Museum of Natural History), 31 (Sinclair Stammers/SPL); Stephen T. Hasiotis: 10, 49; Superstock, Inc.: cover, 37, 45.

Illustrations by Joe LeMonnier and Victory Productions/Craig Roscoe

> Visit Franklin Watts on the Internet at:
> http://publishing.grolier.com

Library of Congress Cataloging-in-Publication Data

Kittinger, Jo S.
    Stories in stone: the world of animal fossils / Jo S. Kittinger.
        p. cm. — (A First book)
    Includes bibliographical references and index.
    Summary: Describes the formation and characteristics of animal fossils, including those of trilobites, lobe-finned fishes, and dinosaurs, and explains how they give us information about the history of the earth.
    ISBN 0-531-20384-0 (lib. bdg.)   0-531-15924-8 (pbk.)
    1. Animals, Fossil—Juvenile literature. [1. Prehistoric animals. 2. Fossils. 3. Paleontology.] I. Title. II. Series.
QE765.K53   1998
560—dc21   98-8029
                                                  CIP
                                                  AC

Contents

Finding fossils is easier than you might think.
This boy found a trilobite fossil at a site in Lansing, New York.

CHAPTER 1

A ROCK SANDWICH

When you dig down into the ground, you come across layers of dirt. Mixed into the dirt are rotting leaves, plant roots, rocks, and all sorts of little creatures. If you look closely at some of the rocks, you might spot a **fossil**. Fossils are common in most parts of the United States, Canada, and many other counties, and they are easier to find than you may think.

If you happen to find large fossil bones, call a professional scientist at a local college or university to collect them. Special care must be taken to preserve such fossils. And if your find is a new **species**, perhaps it will be named after you.

Most people think of fossils as the remains of plants, animals, or other living things that died long ago. But the word "fossil" is also used to describe any evidence of these creatures. You probably know that dinosaur bones are fossils, but you might be surprised to learn that their footprints are fossils, too.

One of the best places to look for fossils is in **sedimentary rock**, such as shale, sandstone, or limestone. This kind of rock forms when layers of **sediments**—mud, sand,

The Grand Canyon in Arizona is a perfect place to see layer upon layer of sedimentary rock.

shells, and other materials—are laid down over a long period of time. To understand how sedimentary rock forms, imagine making a huge sandwich. You would probably start with a slice of bread. Then you might add bologna, ham, turkey, cheese, lettuce, tomatoes, olive and pickle slices, and mayonnaise. Finally, you would add another slice of bread. Sedimentary rock forms in the same way— one layer at a time.

Now imagine placing a heavy bucket of water on top of that sandwich. If you left it there for a long time, the sandwich would be squashed—flattened out. The materials that make up sedimentary rock have been flattened and compressed in this way. Most sedimentary rock was once the floor of a sea, an ocean, a swamp, or a lake. Over thousands of years, the weight of the water and the upper layers of sediments pushed down on the lower layers and turned them into rock.

TYPES OF FOSSILS

The fossils in sedimentary rock are the remains of plants, animals, and other living things that were buried in the layers of sediment. They are similar to the pickle and olive slices in your imaginary sandwich. To fossilize, a creature must be buried soon after it dies—before it is eaten by animals or begins to decay. In most cases, only a creature's hard parts—such as bones, teeth, and shells—fossilize. Once in a while, however, soft tissues—such as skin and muscle—are preserved.

There are many different types of fossils. The fossils that are probably most familiar to you—the kind you usually see at museums—are preserved through a process called **mineralization**. As groundwater comes into contact with buried bones, teeth, and shells, some or all of the original material is washed away and replaced by minerals in the water. The result is a hard, rocklike fossil. This process can take many, many years. Other fossils, called **molds**, are imprints of bones, shells, or other hard body parts. A mold can form if a creature's body lands in mud when it dies.

This rock contains molds of brachniopods.

The animal's body decays, but its outline is left behind when the mud hardens into rock. If you press an object, such as a shell, into wet clay and let it harden for a few hours, you can see what a mold looks like.

Sometimes a mold fills with minerals. When those minerals harden into stone, the resulting fossil is called a **cast**. Scientists sometimes copy molds by making casts with plaster of paris.

8

Trace fossils, like this dinosaur footprint, tell us about an animal's life.

Fossils that are not part of the animal itself are called **trace fossils**. Trace fossils can tell us where and when an animal lived, or reveal something about its behavior. Foot prints are trace fossils, for example. A close examination may reveal the size and weight of the animal, whether it was a good climber, or how it moved—whether it walked, hopped or trotted. **Coprolites**—fossilized animal droppings—can tell us where an animal lived and what it ate.

Believe it or not, tunnels and mounds can also be trace fossils. Tiny tunnels in sedimentary rock may be evidence of ancient worms or clams. **Paleontologists**—scientists who study fossils—have discovered that huge sandstone pillars in New Mexico are actually the remains of ancient termite

This fossilized termite nest in Gallup, New Mexico is similar to modern termite nests in Africa.

nests. These nests are 20 feet (6 m) high and 6 feet (1.8 m) in diameter. They extend 120 feet (36 m) below the ground.

The remains of ancient animals that are not permanently preserved are sometimes called **false fossils**. False fossils include natural **mummies** found in very dry areas, and frozen animals found in the coldest parts of the world. These false fossils can also teach us about ancient creatures. Many natural mummies still have skin and fur, while true fossils do not. Frozen creatures often have soft tissues as well as skin and fur. Because we have found frozen woolly mammoths, we know that these elephant-like animals had humps of fat high on their backs and long, shaggy fur.

WHY DINOSAUR NAMES ARE HARD TO SPELL

Tyrannosaurus rex, *Apatosaurus*, *Triceratops*—these are the names of some familiar dinosaurs. If you've ever visited a museum with dinosaurs on display, you might have noticed their names seem long and are hard to pronounce. And if you've ever written a report about one of these mighty beasts, you probably thought its name was hard to spell. Did you ever wonder why ancient animals never seem to have simple names like "dog," "cat," or "mouse"?

Names like "dog" and "cat" are common names—names we use every day to describe the creatures around us. But scientists use a different naming system because they want to understand how plants, animals, and other living things are related to one another. According to that system, all dogs are called *Canis familiaris*. And since dogs are closely related to wolves, they have similar scientific names. Scientists all over the world call wolves *Canis lupus*. The scientific name for coyotes, which also look and act like dogs, is *Canis latrans*.

This system of naming creatures according to they way they look and act was developed by a Swedish botanist named Carolus Linnaeus in the 1700s. Scientific names are made up of Latin words because, in those days, all well-educated people learned Latin as well as their own language. As a result, the use of scientific names has made it possible for scientists all over the world to know that they were talking about the same creature.

We do not see fossilized creatures around us all the time, so they are almost never given common names. Like scientists, we call them by their Latin scientific names. That's why they can be so hard to spell!

Whenever a new type of creature is identified, the person who discovered the first fossils is usually allowed to give it a scientific name. *Tyrannosaurus rex* is a scientific name that means "king of the tyrant lizards." Sometimes a creature is named more than once by mistake. When that happens, the earliest name is considered the official name. Have you ever heard of *Brontosaurus,* a dinosaur named in 1879? Fossils of the same dinosaur were named *Apatosaurus* in 1877. *Apatosaurus* is, therefore, the correct scientific name.

HOW OLD IS THAT FOSSIL?

When paleontologists discover a new fossil, the first thing they try to find out is how old it is. Is the fossil 600 million

This beast has two names—*Apatosaurus* and *Brontosaurus*.
Which is correct?

Geologic Time Scale

TIME (Millions of years ago)	ERA	PERIOD	DOMINANT ANIMAL LIFE
1.8 to present	Cenozoic	Quaternary	Mammals
65 to 1.8	Cenozoic	Tertiary	
146 to 65	Mesozoic	Cretaceous	Dinosaurs
208 to 146	Mesozoic	Jurassic	
245 to 208	Mesozoic	Triassic	
286 to 245	Paleozoic	Permian	Early reptiles
360 to 286	Paleozoic	Carboniferous	Amphibians
410 to 360	Paleozoic	Devonian	Fishes
440 to 410	Paleozoic	Silurian	
505 to 440	Paleozoic	Ordovician	Early ocean animals
544 to 505	Paleozoic	Cambrian	

14

years old or just 10,000 years old? To answer this question, scientists examine the sample closely and look for clues. First, they look at the rock the fossil was found in. Did the fossil come from a bottom layer or a top layer? The bottom layers were laid down first, so a fossil at the bottom would be older than a fossil at the top.

To estimate a fossil's **relative age**, paleontologists look at other fossils in the rock. They know that certain creatures lived on Earth during a particular time period and then became **extinct**. If the fossil they have just uncovered is found in the same layer of rock as a known fossil species, the scientists know that both creatures lived at the same time. To determine a fossil's **absolute age**, paleontologists do laboratory tests to find out how old the rocks that contain the fossil are.

Because scientists also want to know what life was like on Earth when a certain animal lived and what other animals were alive at the same time, they divide the last 600 million years—the time they believe animals have existed on Earth—into three distinct periods of time called **eras**. As you can see by looking at the **geologic time scale** on page 14, each of these eras is subdivided into two or more periods. When paleontologists describe a particular fossil, they might say that it lived during the early Devonian period. Other scientists would then know that the animal lived about 360 to 410 million years ago according to this scale.

CHAPTER 2

BURIED AT SEA

The earliest animals on Earth lived in the ocean and were closely related to the sponges, corals, clams, lobsters, horseshoe crabs, and water fleas found in the ocean today. You might expect to find fossils of these ocean dwellers only in rock below the seafloor, but they are found in all sorts of places—on mountaintops, in the middle of grasslands, and even in deserts. How did fossils of ocean animals end up there? At one time, all these places were underwater.

Fossils tell us a lot about what Earth was like long ago. By studying fossils, scientists have learned that the ancestors of creatures now found in Central America once lived in the northern parts of the United States and Canada. This means that North Dakota was once as warm as Guatemala is today.

Along with discoveries made by geologists—scientists who study rocks—fossil evidence shows that the continents are moving very slowly. At one time, all the land on Earth apparently existed as one giant continent called Pangaea. The continents are still moving today—at about the same rate as your fingernails grow. Each year, the

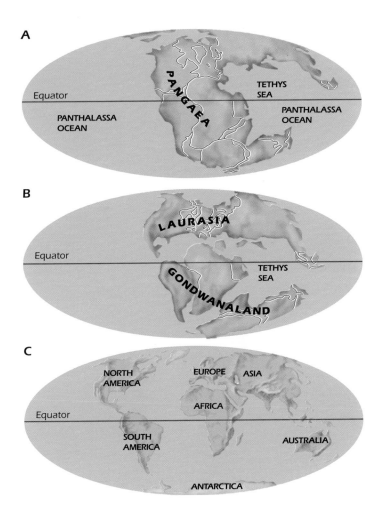

Scientists believe that, about 180 million years ago, Earth had one huge continent—called Pangaea—surrounded by a large ocean (A). Over the next 60 million years, Pangaea split into two land masses—Laurasia and Gondwanaland (B). As time continues to pass, the land broke into several more pieces. Today, there are seven continents (C).

Each of these "Xs" was once a living colony of graptolites.

A polished Petoskey stone (left) and a fossilized *Hexogonaria* coral (right).

Atlantic Ocean gets a little larger and the Pacific Ocean gets a little smaller.

As the continents move, lakes, rivers, and oceans form and then disappear. So the fossil of an animal that once lived in the ocean may be found in a desert today. Many different fossils of simple ocean animals have been uncovered by paleontologists. Some are easily identifiable as the ancestors of animals we know today. Others are so small or unimpressive that many people might not notice them at all.

GRAPTOLITES

These tiny animals lived in large groups and often formed lines that look like scratch marks. You shouldn't be surprised to find out that the word "graptolite" means "writing on rock." Sometimes, graptolite colonies formed familiar shapes or letters. One kind, called *Tetragraptus*, often lived in colonies that looked like the letter X.

Graptolites are common in rocks dating to the Ordovician, Silurian, and early Devonian periods. Paleontologists often use them to determine the ages of other fossils in a particular rock sample.

CORALS

Today, living corals are found in reefs off the coast of Hawaii and along many other tropical coasts. Fossils of ancient corals are found all over the world, too. Several species of fossilized corals, called Petoskey stones, are so common in Michigan that they have been named the official state stone. If you look closely at polished Petoskey stones, you will see six-sided structures. These stones were once colonies of corals.

Like graptolites, corals are small animals that live in large groups. Each individual animal has stinging tentacles that it uses to catch food and defend itself against enemies.

TRILOBITES

You may have seen a trilobite fossil at a museum or in a book. The fossils of these animals, which are related to crabs and lobsters, are very common. The word "trilobite" means "three lobes." A trilobite's body has three parts—a head, a **thorax**, and a tail. If you look closely, you will see that the thorax is divided into three vertical sections, or lobes, that run down the body. You will also see that many horizontal segments run across the body. These segments made it possible for the animal to curl up into a tight ball like a pillbug. Sometimes scientists find trilobite fossils in this rolled-up position.

More than 10,000 species of trilobite fossils have been identified. Although most are less than 4 inches (10 cm) long, some are much larger. Fossils of *Paradoxides harlani* may be up to 19 inches (48 cm) long and 12 inches (30 cm) wide.

Like crabs and lobsters, trilobites had a hard shell-like covering called an **exoskeleton**. As trilobites grew, they shed their shell several times. Paleontologists have found many fossils of discarded exoskeletons. Because the animals did not die in these shells, they are considered trace

These *Phacops* trilobites lived during the Devonian period.

fossils. Trilobites also left behind other trace fossils—their trackways. Because trilobites flourished throughout the Paleozoic era, paleontologists often use them to help determine the age of other fossils found in the same layer of rock.

SEA STARS AND BRITTLE STARS
Both of these animals first appeared during the Ordovician period—and still survive today. While sea stars have

Plant or animal? It's no suprise that crinoids are commonly called sea lilies.

broad arms and look like a star, brittle stars have a round center and slender, snake-like arms. Fossils of these animals are less common than trilobite fossils because sea stars and brittles stars have no hard outer coverings.

During the middle Silurian period, a small sea star called *Hudsonaster* was common off the coast of North America. It was about 1 inch (2.5 cm) across and had five stubby triangular arms.

CRINOIDS

Crinoid fossils are much more common than sea star fossils. These animals are also called "sea lilies" because they live on a stem and have a flower-like body. The stems, which are surrounded by a protective limestone shell, were preserved more often than the bodies.

Crinoids first appeared in the early Ordovician period, and can be found in Paleozoic rocks throughout North America. In some places, huge quantities of crinoid skeletons piled up to create incredible limestone formations.

OCEAN SNAILS

Some of the most beautiful shells in the world are those of ocean snails. Their fossils are beautiful, too. *Busycon*, a type of whelk, has been common along the coasts of North America since the Cretaceous period. The shell of a *Busycon* may be up to 5 inches (13 cm) long and $2\frac{1}{4}$ inches (6 cm) wide. In most animals with shells, the shells curl to either the right or the left, but *Busycon* shells can coil in either direction.

AMMONITES

Although these animals have been extinct since the end of the Cretaceous period, their fossils are not that hard to find. Ammonites are named for Ammon, an Egyptian god with the horns of a ram and the body of a man. Most ammonites have tightly coiled shells that look like a ram's horns. In many cases, the shells are ornamented with bumps, ribs, or spines.

Dactylioceras ammonites fill this slab of Jurassic rock.

A modern *Nautilus* shell—whole and sliced open—
has much in common with a fossil of *Titanoceras*.
The straight nautiloid fossils in this photograph
are *Orthoceras*.

Ammonite shells may have squiggly marks called **suture lines**. These sutures sometimes form intricate patterns that show where two chambers of the shell met. Each type of ammonite has its own pattern of sutures.

The inside of every ammonite shell is divided into chambers. Over time, as the shell becomes a fossil, these chambers sometimes fill with crystallized minerals. When these beautiful specimens are cut and polished, you can see the chambers inside.

Because many types of ammonites became extinct soon after they appear in the fossils record, paleontologists can use them to determine the relative age of other fossils. For example, *Meekoceras* lived only during the late Triassic period, and *Prinocyclus* existed only during the middle Cretaceous period.

NAUTILOIDS

Like ammonites, nautiloids have chambered shells that may be either straight or coiled. Some nautiloid shells also have suture lines. Paleontologists have identified more than 2,000 different kinds of nautiloid fossils, but only one type of nautiloid is living today. It is called the *Nautilus*.

CLAMS, OYSTERS, SCALLOPS, AND MUSSELS

The earliest relatives of these animals lived during the Cambrian period. Their fossils are common during every period of geologic time for two reasons: Their thick, solid shells are perfectly suited for mineralization; and these

Both halves of a bivalve shell (left) match perfectly, but the two halves of a brachiopod shell (right) are quite different.

animals often burrow in the sand, so many are already buried when they die.

Chesapecten, which lived during the late Tertiary period, was the first North American fossil to be described and illustrated. In 1687, Martin Lister published a drawing and description of this scallop-shaped shell. *Chesapecten*, which has a large, heavy shell, is named after the Chesapeake Bay, Maryland, where it is abundant.

BRACHIOPODS

When you look at a brachiopod, you might think it's a clam or a scallop, but the animal inside is quite different. If you compare the shells of a clam and a brachiopod, you will see that the two halves of a clam's shell are almost exactly the same, while the two halves of a brachiopod's shell do not match.

Herbertella ,which was a widespread brachiopod in eastern North America during the Ordovician period, was about $1\frac{1}{4}$ inches (3.2 cm) long and $1\frac{3}{4}$ inches (4.4 cm) wide. It had a groove on the bottom half of its shell and a hump on the top half. Brachiopods were as plentiful in the Paleozoic seas as clams and mussels are in our waters today.

CHAPTER 3

SWIMMERS IN THE SAND

THE EARLIEST FISHES

Most scientists believe that jawless fishes with thick, bony plates were the first animals to develop backbones. By the Devonian period, nearly all of these agnathans had died out. (Two groups of jawless fishes still survive today—lampreys and hagfish.)

Agnathans were replaced by jawed fishes called placoderms. The earliest fossils of placoderms appeared in rock from the Silurian period. One of the largest Paleozoic animals was a placoderm called *Dunkleosteus*. This fierce-looking fish was 30 feet (9 m) long and had an armored head and enormous jaws.

THE FIRST SHARKS

Another group of fishes—sharks, rays, and skates—appeared soon after placoderms. The great white shark (*Carcharodon carcharias*) is the most fearsome fish alive today, but an extinct relative—*Carcharodon megalodon*—was even more terrifying. It was 40 to 50 feet (12 to 15 m) long, and its mouth was so large that a small car could drive

Dunkleosteus was a fearsome fish, judging from this skull fossil.

through its giant fossilized jaws. The driver would have to be very careful, though. It would be easy to get a flat tire on all those sharp teeth. Each tooth was 6 to 8 inches (15 to 20 cm) long. *Carcharodon* teeth from the Middle Tertiary through early Quaternary periods have been found all over the world. In the United States, you can find them in North and South Carolina.

Because shark skeletons are made of **cartilage** instead of bone, their teeth are usually the only remains that fossilize. Small shark teeth are among the most common fossils on Earth.

THE RISE OF BONY FISHES

Although sharks and their relatives still exist today, there are far fewer than at earlier times in Earth's history. Today, the largest group of fish on Earth are the bony fishes—trout, catfish, perch, bass, cod, flounder, tuna, and most other freshwater and saltwater fish.

There are two groups of bony fishes—lobe-finned fishes and ray-finned fishes. The first lobe-finned fishes appeared during the Devonian period. Although they were once abundant in the world's oceans, only a few survive today, including six kinds of lungfishes. The only other surviving lobe-finned fish is *Coelacanthia hatimeria*. Scientists thought this fish was extinct until one was caught off the coast of South Africa in 1938!

Ray-finned fishes are much more common. They thrive in oceans, rivers, and lakes all over the world today, and they were abundant in prehistoric times, too. Some of the

A school of fossilized fish are easy to spot in this rock from the Green River Formation in Wyoming.

best-preserved fish fossils have been found in rocky limestone and pink shale cliffs in Wyoming, Utah, and Colorado. At one time, this area, known as the Green River Formation, was covered by a great lake. Today the rocks contain thousands of molds—fins, scales, and complete skeletons—of the fish that once lived in that lake. Fossils of *Mioplosus*, *Diplomystus*, and *Knightia* are easy to spot here.

Mosaurs, like this one, were huge ocean reptiles. This skeleton was found in Kansas, far from today's oceans.

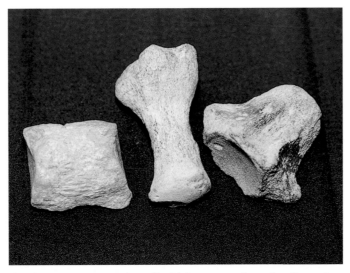

A plesiosaur vertebra (left) is cupped on both ends. Mosasaur vertebrae (center and right) are cupped on one end and rounded on the other.

ANCIENT REPTILES OF THE SEA

If you could go back in time and fish in an ancient ocean, you might hook something other than a fish. Believe it or not, giant **reptiles** once roamed the oceans. Mosasaurs, huge beasts that reached lengths of 55 feet (16.5 m), swam through the Cretaceous seas. Today, segments of mosasaur backbones, called **vertebrae**, are often found in the Mooreville Chalk of Alabama. These fossils are easy to identify. Each is cupped on one end and rounded on the other. Can you picture how they fit together?

Plesiosaurs were also common in ancient oceans. These reptiles had very long necks, pudgy bodies, and four paddle-shaped flippers. Their fossils—especially vertebrae—are

This *Basilosaurus cetoides* skeleton is on display at the Smithsonian's Museum of Natural History.

found in rocks dating from the Triassic, Jurassic, and Cretaceous periods. It isn't too difficult to tell the difference between the vertebrae of plesiosaurs and mosasaurs. In plesiosaurs, the vertebrae are cupped on both ends.

ANCIENT OCEAN MAMMALS

Strange **mammals** swam in Earth's oceans during the Tertiary period. In 1832, Richard Harlan found twenty-eight large vertebrae fossils in Louisiana. At first, he thought he had discovered the remains of a huge reptile, but as Harlan uncovered additional bones, it became clear that he was looking at the remains of *Basilosaurus cetoides*—a very long, slender mammal with fins. This animal is commonly referred to as a zeuglodon.

A few years later, several nearly complete skeletons of zeuglodons were exposed in a field in Alabama. Some people thought the zeuglodon, which can be 70 feet (21 m) long, must have been a type of sea serpent. In 1984, Alabama adopted the *Basilosaurus* as its state fossil. You can see a skeleton of this ancient animal at the Smithsonian's Museum of Natural History in Washington, D.C.

CHAPTER 4

THE TERRIBLE LIZARDS

You have grown up knowing that dinosaurs existed, but people did not always know about them. By the 1800s, people had discovered enough fossils of dinosaur bones and teeth to know that monstrous reptiles had once roamed the earth. In 1841, a British scientist named Sir Richard Owen named the creatures "dinosaurs," which means "terrible lizards." But dinosaurs were not really terrible, and they were not lizards at all!

At the time Owen lived, very little was known about dinosaurs. In fact, some people thought they might still exist. Today we know that dinosaurs dominated life on land during the Mesozoic era. How many types of dinosaurs can you name? More than 60 different kinds have been identified in the United States. Worldwide, there may have been as many as 500 different species.

RECONSTRUCTING THE PAST

Even though many different dinosaurs existed, chances are, you will never find an entire dinosaur skeleton. When a dinosaur died, its flesh was usually eaten by other crea-

Paleontologists believe this is what *Tyrannosaurus rex* fossils would look like fully dressed.

Fossils, like this hatchling *Maiasaurus*, tell us that dinosaurs laid eggs.

tures. Even if the animal's body decayed naturally, its bones were probably scattered before sediments covered them.

Whenever paleontologists find a jumble of dinosaur bones, they try to figure out how they fit together. It's sort of like trying to do a giant jigsaw puzzle. Have you ever put a puzzle piece in the wrong place? Sometimes scientists make this mistake, too. When scientists were trying to put together the bones of *Iguanodon*—the first dinosaur discovered—they decided that one of the bones was a horn. Later, they realized the piece was actually a thumb spike. Many other mistakes were made, too. In one case, scientists accidentally put the head of one type of dinosaur on the body of another type of dinosaur.

Today we have a number of remarkable skeletons that are nearly complete as well as many others that give us enough information to picture the entire animal. Some fossils show us things we thought we'd never know, such as the texture of dinosaur skin. These molds, which were made when mud hardened soon after the animal's death, look a lot like the skin of some modern lizards. Other fossils provide important clues about the dinosaurs' lives. The preserved contents of a duckbill's stomach, eggs containing baby dinosaurs, bite marks on bones from dinosaur battles, and the trackways of dinosaur footprints—these tell us far more than a leg bone or vertebra ever could.

To identify a dinosaur skeleton, scientists must first look at its hipbones. Dinosaurs are divided into two main groups—saurischians and ornithischians—based on the way that three bones fit together to form the hip. It is also important to examine the dinosaur's teeth and toes. Most saurischians had long teeth and clawed feet. The teeth of ornithischians were often smaller and blunt. In addition, many ornithischians had a horny beak instead of front teeth. All ornithischians had hooves attached to each toe.

A Look at Saurischians

Scientists divide saurischians into two subgroups— theropods and sauropods. Theropods had bird-like feet, walked on two legs, and ate meat. Most had short front arms with clawed hands. Like modern lizards, sauropods had feet with five toes. But they were much bigger than the lizards we see today. Sauropods had huge bodies, long necks, and long tails. Unlike theropods, they ate plants and stood on four legs as big as tree trunks. Sauropods lived from the early Jurassic period to the end of the Cretaceous period. Their fossils have been found on every continent except Antarctica.

Theropods

Tyrannosaurus rex is the most famous theropod. It was a fierce hunter with huge jaws and sixty sharp teeth up to 6 inches (15 cm) long. *T. rex* lived during the late Cretaceous period, but if it were alive today, it easily could peek in your upstairs windows and grab you out of bed. *T. rex* stood $18\frac{1}{2}$ feet (5.6 m) tall and was longer than a school bus.

Coelophysis, a 10-foot (3-m) long theropod with a whip-like tail, lived during the Triassic period. This little dinosaur created a big stir in 1947 when Edwin H. Colbert

40

T. rex had a massive skull and huge teeth.

Cast of a complete *Coelophysis* skeleton from Ghost Ranch, New Mexico

discovered more than twenty of them at Ghost Ranch in New Mexico. *Coelophysis* means "hollow form" in Greek. The bones of these dinosaurs were hollow—like those of a bird. (Some scientists think these fossils might belong to a group of dinosaurs called *Rioarribasaurus,* rather than *Coelophysis.* You can stay up to date with this debate by searching for their names on the World Wide Web.)

Two *Coelophysis* skeletons were found with the remains of tiny *Coelophysis* bones inside their rib cage. Some scientists thought this meant that *Coelophysis* gave birth to live young. Based on the size of the young *Coelophysis*, however, it is more likely that the adults were **cannibals** and ate the babies after they hatched. Another group of skeletons showed that large numbers of *Coelophysis* of all ages lived in herds. As a result, many paleontologists believe that the adults may have cared for their young.

Sauropods

Brachiosaurus, one of the heaviest sauropods, tipped the scale at 70 to 80 tons. By comparison, an elephant weighs about 5 tons. And some dinosaurs may have been even heavier. Have you ever heard of Ultrasaurus? It is the common name used to describe a dinosaur that had a 9-foot (2.7-m)-wide shoulder blade and 5-foot (1.5-m)-long vertebrae. Its fossils suggest that the beast was more than 98 feet (30 m) long. That's one-third larger than *Brachiosaurus*! (This dinosaur does not yet have a scientific name because not enough bones have been found to classify it.)

Some paleontologists believe Ultrasaurus may just be a gigantic *Brachiosaurus.* Because the fossils are so much larger than *Brachiosaurus* fossils, scientists think that some dinosaurs may have continued to grow after they became adults. This idea is not totally new. One group of modern reptiles—the alligators—are known to continue growing all their lives.

Not all sauropods are as large as *Brachiosaurus*. One example is the tiny *Mussaurus,* which means "mouse lizard." The smallest dinosaur ever found was the skeleton of a baby *Mussaurus* discovered in a nest at a late Triassic site in Argentina. Only 8 inches (20 cm) long, the entire skeleton could fit in your hands.

A LOOK AT ORNITHISCHIANS

Paleontologists divide ornithischians into five subgroups—ornithopods, ankylosaurs, stegosaurs, pachycephalosaurs, and ceratopsians. Some stood on all four feet, while others stood on only two. During the Triassic, Jurassic, and Cretaceous periods, ornithischians lived all over the world. Although nearly all ornithischians ate plants, they came in a variety of sizes. Some were no larger than a puppy, while others were 40 feet (12 m) long. A few of the least-known ornithischians are discussed in the next two sections.

Pachycephalosaurs

You may already know something about ornithopods and ankylosaurs, and you almost certainly are familiar with stegosaurs, but have you ever heard of the pachycephalosaurs? The word "pachycephalosaur" means "thick-headed lizard." The brain of this dinosaur was encased in a helmet of bone up to 9 inches (23 cm) thick. Its snout and the back of its skull were covered with bumps and short spikes. Can you picture two of these dinosaurs ramming each other like football players?

Although scientists have not found an entire skeleton of the pachycephalosaur called *Stygimoloch*, it appears that this small dinosaur had a crown full of horns. Found in Late Cretaceous deposits in Montana, *Stygimoloch* sported three or four spikes surrounded by a cluster of bony bumps

Pachycephalosaurs had very thick skulls.

This *Einiosaurus* skull features a "can-opener" shaped nose horn and a bony frill behind the head.

on each side of its head. The longest spike was 4 inches (10 cm) in length. That's very impressive for a dinosaur only 7 feet (2 m) long, including the tail. This evil-looking reptile was named for the mythological River Styx and for Moloch, an ancient god worshiped with human sacrifices.

Ceratopsians

The word "ceratops" means "horned dinosaur." In 1994, two new types of ceratopsians were discovered in Montana. These dinosaurs, named *Einiosaurus* and *Achelousaurus,* were found in rock dating to the early Cretaceous period. Both dinosaurs had two spikes jutting from a frill behind the head.

The name *Einiosaurus*, meaning "buffalo lizard," refers to the idea that the ceratopsians lived in large herds like buffalo. *Einiosaurus* had low, rounded horns just above their eyes. Some had a hooked "can-opener" nose horn. *Achelousaurus* did not have true horns, but they did have lumpy mounds above their eyes and on their snouts.

CHAPTER 5

FURS AND FEATHERS, BONES AND TEETH

According to fossil evidence, birds and land mammals first appeared during the Mesozoic era. However, it wasn't until after the great extinction of dinosaurs at the end of the Cretaceous period that mammals began to dominate the land. Scientists have discovered fossils of many incredible beasts, such as woolly rhinos and saber-toothed cats, in rock dating to the Tertiary period. Bird fossils are much more rare, probably because their hollow bones are fragile.

THE OLDEST BIRDS

The oldest-known bird lived during the Jurassic period. A single fossilized feather of this bird, which is called *Archaeopteryx*, was discovered in 1860. The name *Archaeopteryx* means "ancient wing."

In 1861, a nearly complete *Archaeopteryx* fossil was found in a quarry near Solenhofen, Germany. Paleontologists were excited to see its feathers and skeleton imprinted on a slab of limestone. If the image of feathers had not been preserved, *Archaeopteryx* might have been clas-

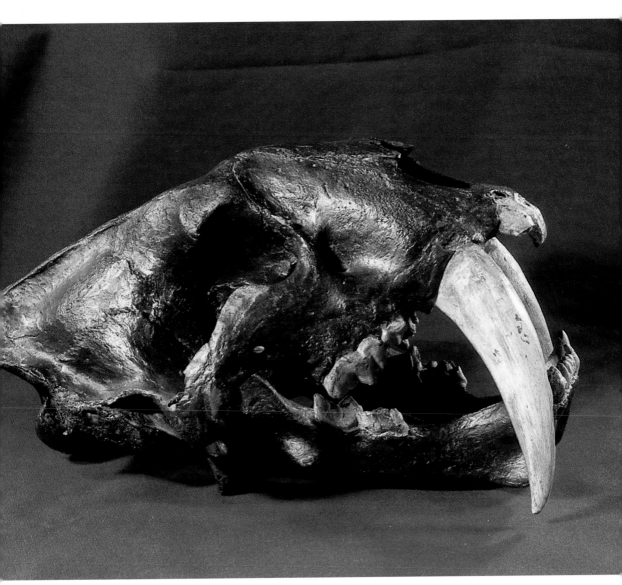

This saber-toothed cat skull was pulled from the La Brea tar pits in California.

This rare fossil captured the bones and feathers of *Archaeopteryx*, the oldest known bird.

sified as a reptile. Unlike today's birds, the animal had teeth, claws on its wings, and a long bony tail.

Confuciusornis sanctus is a species of extinct bird found in China. It was named in honor of the Chinese philosopher Confucius. This toothless bird was slightly younger than *Archaeopteryx*—it lived during the early Cretaceous period.

Scientists found many *Confuciusornis sanctus* skeletons in one small area. What do you think that might mean? Paleontologists believe it is the first evidence of birds living in colonies. Another surprise was the discovery of modern-type bird fossils in the same rock deposits. This means that ancient and modern-type birds were living side by side.

More recently, a farmer living in the Liaoning Province of China discovered another ancient bird fossil. Although this sparrow-sized bird—called *Liaoningornis*—was probably only a little younger than *Archaeopteryx*, its wings and tail were much more like those of modern birds.

Scientists disagree about the age of the rocks this skeleton came from. Some say they were deposited in the late Jurassic period, while others think these rocks date to the early Cretaceous period. If these birds did live during the late Jurassic period, *Liaoningornis* was alive at about the same time as *Archaeopteryx*.

In 1996, a Spanish paleontologist discovered a wonderfully preserved bird fossil. The new bird, named *Eoalulavis hoyasi*, was about the size of a goldfinch and came with a bellyful of surprises. By studying its stomach, scientists could tell what the bird had eaten for dinner. *Eoalulavis hoyasi* has been dated to the early Cretaceous period. It is the earliest bird fossil with wings like those of modern flying birds. Fossil evidence suggests that all modern birds existed by the end of the Tertiary period.

THE RISE OF MAMMALS

You probably get excited when you spot a deer running across an open field or see a raccoon's eyes glowing at night, but just try to imagine what it would be like to encounter some of the mammals that once lived in North America. There were mammoths, mastodons, giant ground sloths, saber-toothed cats, and many others. Today these animals exist only as fossils.

One of the best sources of the fossils of ancient mammals is the La Brea tar pits in southern California. These large puddles of sticky, black tar formed during the early Quaternary period when oil seeped up onto land and partially dried into tar. As rain fell, it pooled on the surface of the tar. When animals came to drink this water, they often became trapped in the thick, sticky tar. More animals were attracted because they wanted to eat the remains of the dead animals. They, too, became trapped in the tar. Bones of giant ground sloths, saber-toothed cats, extinct horses, and mammoths have all been pulled from the tar.

As you may know, police sometimes use dental records to identify murder victims. Similarly, scientists rely on teeth, especially **molars**, to identify the skeletons of ancient mammals. In fact, modern paleontologists have a name for almost every crinkle and point of a mammal tooth.

52

The La Brea tar pits trapped a wide variety of prehistoric animals.

Mammoth or Mastodon?

Do you know the difference between a mammoth and a mastodon? Thomas Jefferson didn't. While he was president, he sent the French government some fossilized mastodon bones as a gift. In his letter, however, he called them "mammoth bones." This mistake isn't hard to make—both animals were related to elephants and had shaggy coats.

If Jefferson had looked closely at the animal's tusks and teeth, he would have known that the fossil was a mastodon.

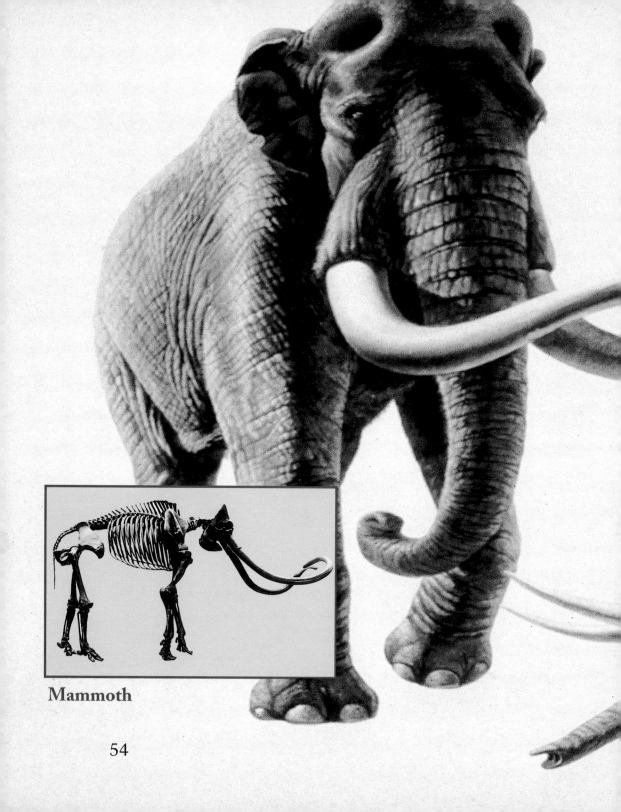

Mammoth

What's the difference between a mammoth and a mastodon? As you can see from these drawings and skeleton models, the easiest way to tell these giant elephant-like animals apart is by looking at their tusks.

Mastodon

Prehistoric cave artists painted the mammoth with mighty tusks that curved away from each other, then back again. In some cases, they made a complete circle, with the tips crossing. Their teeth were flat grinders with ridges across the top for chewing grass.

Mammoth fossils are quite common, and have been found throughout North America. *Mammuthus imperator,* the imperial mammoth, was the largest elephant that ever lived. It stood 14 to 15 feet (4 to 4.5 m) high at the shoulder—that's as tall as two basketball players!

Mastodons had long, upward-curving tusks. Their teeth had rows of rounded knobs for crushing leaves. Although mastodons are extinct today, about 100 different kinds once lived on Earth.

Jefferson sent bones of *Mastodon americanis* to France. Fossils of this animal were first discovered near the Ohio River in Kentucky in 1705. The mastodon bones sent to France had been collected at Big Bone Lick, a site in Kentucky. The dig, which Jefferson funded, was carried out by William Clark, who is best known for exploring the western United States with Meriwether Lewis.

Giant Ground Sloth

Jefferson was very interested in fossils. In fact, one ancient animal was named after him. *Megalonyx jeffersonii* was a giant ground sloth that lived in North America. Other common ground sloths included *Megatherium,* which was bigger than any elephant alive today, and *Glossotherium,* which was a little smaller.

Fossils of giant ground sloths show the animals were as big as modern elephants.

Glossary

absolute age—the age of rock as determined by tests on the rock itself.

cannibal—an animal that eats other members of its species.

cartilage—a tough, elastic tissue.

cast—a fossil formed when mud or minerals harden inside a mold.

coprolite—fossilized droppings, or animal waste.

era—a span of geologic time that contains several periods.

exoskeleton—the tough, skinlike outer layer of lobsters, crabs, insects, and related animals.

extinct—the dying out of a species.

false fossil—the remains of ancient animals that are not permanently preserved.

fossil—the preserved remains or evidence of ancient life.

geologic time scale—a division of time into various layers of Earth in which distinctive fossils are found, and the assignment of time periods to those divisions.

mammal—a member of the group of animals that includes bears, cats, dogs, whales, and humans. A mammal has a backbone and feeds its young with mother's milk.

mineralization—a process by which bone, shells, teeth, and other hard body parts are transformed into rock-hard fossils.

molar—a tooth with a rounded or flattened surface. A person has twelve molars at the back of his or her mouth (six on top and six on the bottom).

mold—a hollow impression in rock that shows the shape of a shell, bone, or other part of a living thing.

mummy—the remains of an animal that are somewhat preserved by drying.

paleontologist—a scientist who studies prehistoric life through fossils.

relative age—the age of rock determined by what type of fossils it contains.

reptile—a member of the group of animals that includes crocodiles, alligators, turtles, snakes, and lizards. A reptile has a backbone and is cold-blooded.

sediment—tiny bits of mud, sand, or other rock material often carried by water.

sedimentary rock—rock made from layers of sand, mud, or other material that have hardened.

species—a group of creatures within a genus that share certain characteristics. Members of the same species can mate and produce young.

suture lines—lines on an ammonite or nautiloid fossil, showing where two chambers meet inside.

thorax—the middle body segment of lobsters, crabs, insects, and related animals.

trace fossil—a preserved record of animal activity, such as tracks, burrows, or coprolites.

vertebra (*pl* vertebrae) —a bony segment of the backbone.

For More Information

BOOKS

Benton, Michael. *Focus on Dinosaurs.* New York: Gloucester Press, Aladdin Books, 1993.

Dixon, Dougal. *Dinosaurs: The Fossil Hunters.* Jackson, TN: Davidson Titles, Inc., 1994.

Dixon, Dougal and Rupert Matthews. *The Illustrated Encyclopedia of Prehistoric Life.* New York: Smithmark, 1992.

Gaffney, Eugene S. *Dinosaurs.* New York: Golden Press, 1991.

Lessem, Don and Donald F. Glut. *Dinosaur Encyclopedia.* New York: Random House, 1993.

Pellant, Chris. *Fossils of the World.* San Diego, CA: Thunder Bay Press, 1994.

Walker, Cyril and David Ward. *Eyewitness Handbooks: Fossils.* New York: Dorling, Kindersley, Inc., 1992.

WEB SITES

The Arizona Sedimentary Geology and Paleontology Resource has information about fossil sites, geologic formations, and identification of fossils. You can view a variety of fossilized bones, molds and casts, and trace fossils.
http://www.PSIAZ.com/Schur/azpaleo/paleo.html

Collecting Fossils in California lists sites and gives directions to fossil-collecting sites all over California. There is also a link to various news agencies, so you can get the most up-to-date information about fossil finds all over the world.
http://www.gtlsys.com

Fossils of New Jersey features a variety of photos and information about plant and animal fossils from the Cretaceous and Tertiary periods.
http://www.yahoo.com/Science/Earth_Sciences/Paleontology/Fossils/

Kansas Fossils includes photos and descriptions of various trace fossils and bones and molds of simple ocean animals, fish, amphibians, reptiles, mammals, and plants. The site also has a link to a representation of the geologic time scale.
http://cadvantage.com/~leiszler/

Pennsylvania Paleopage has information about Pennsylvania's geological prehistory. It includes descriptions of what life on Earth was like during certain periods and photos and descriptions of various fossils.
http://members.aol.com/jmfabiny/index.html

This site describes and shows photos of dinosaur trackways in Massachusetts.
http://members.aol.com/dinoprints/index.html

Index

Italicized page numbers indicate illustrations.

About the Author

Jo S. Kittinger grew up with a love for creation and books. She studies art and science in college and see them as intertwined. Clay from the earth becomes a vase on her potter's wheel and art is revealed in the fossils she finds. In addition to her writing, Jo works on *The Flicker* children's magazine. Other books by Jo S. Kittinger include *Dead Log Alive!*, *A Look at Rocks*, and *A Look at Minerals*. She lives in Hoover, Alabama, with her rock-hound husband, three children, and an assortment of pets.